Lowcountry Moonshine Chief

FAYE MCKENZIE WITH TOM PILGRIM

authorHOUSE®

AuthorHouse™
1663 Liberty Drive
Bloomington, IN 47403
www.authorhouse.com
Phone: 833-262-8899

This book is a work of non-fiction. Unless otherwise noted, the author and the publisher make no explicit guarantees as to the accuracy of the information contained in this book and in some cases, names of people and places have been altered to protect their privacy.

Published by AuthorHouse 04/27/2021

ISBN: 978-1-6655-2429-2 (sc)
ISBN: 978-1-6655-2428-5 (hc)
ISBN: 978-1-6655-2427-8 (e)

Library of Congress Control Number: 2021908506

Print information available on the last page.

This book is printed on acid-free paper.

Contents

Dedicated To

My Two Sisters in Law
Alberta McKenzie
Sallie Mae McKenzie

Foreword

The low country of South Carolina is that wide area along the Savannah River and the coast, now made more famous by the development of Hilton Head and the quaint homes in the city of Beaufort. This book is the story of other times which were more simple and some of the people who lived in those times. Their lives were at some points simple and at other times very complicated. There was both joy and tragedy.

The focus of this book is a man named Lawrence Earl McKenzie, better known as Chief. He spent his life in the lowcountry. The words on these pages tell of his times and his deeds which had an impact on all of us who knew him.

Mitchell Levy and Bertie McKenzie

One

"We talk about equal opportunity today, but there was some way back in the thirties and forties," said Danny McKenzie. He was a member of the County Commission, Jasper County, South Carolina, and had been asked to speak to a group of businessmen and businesswomen. It was 1987, and this was the yearly presentation of the Commission to business and property owners.

"My step-grandfather was Chief McKenzie. He was the first man to pay women the same wages as men got. He ran moonshine to Savannah and other places. There was one dirt road, the old Charleston Road. Revenue agents would wait along that road looking for moonshine runners. They always were looking for male drivers. But Chief paid women to drive the cars. The agents never stopped women. They would just wave them on through. So, he was the first equal opportunity employer, a man far ahead of his time."

When the laughter ceased and the room settled down Danny McKenzie continued his presentation on the progress of Jasper County.

⁓

Jasper County, South Carolina sits across the Savannah River from the city of Savannah, Georgia. It covers an area of 699 square miles, 655 in land

and 44 in water. It was founded in the year 1912, and was carved out of two counties, Hampton County and Beaufort County.

That area was the home of Yamassee and Coosaw Indians. The first white settlers were Swiss Palantines and French Huguenots. In 1732 Swiss and German immigrants led by Jean Pierre Purry settled along the Savannah River. Other settlers came there, and established rice plantations.

The County was named after Sergeant William Jasper, 1750-1779. He served during the American Revolution with Major Francis Marion in the Second South Carolina Regiment during the first defense of Charleston in June, 1776. During the siege of Savannah, September 16-17, 1779, he saw the flag was struck down. He lifted it up and was killed.

During the War Between The States the Confederate Army defeated the Yankees at the Battle of Honey Hill, November 30, 1864.

Notable citizens of that area include Thomas Heywood, Jr., 1746-1809, who signed the Declaration of Independence, and Henry Martyn Roberts, 1837-1923, author of Roberts Rules of Order.

In the year 1920, in the first census after Jasper County was established, the population was 9,868. Ten years later it had grown by only twenty reaching 9,888.

During the first half of the twentieth century the economy of Jasper County was based on forest products such as lumber from sawmills, turpentine, and agriculture, row crops, vegetables, and livestock.

Along the river there are marsh-lands, savannas, and swamps. The swamps contain bear, deer, and various small animals. Also, the river area lies in a major flight pattern for ducks and geese in the Spring and Fall. There is now a wild-life refuge where these flocks stop on their way to and from their winter residences.

The land is flat, the dirt is black, pine trees and palmettos grow everywhere. When the rains come water stands with no place for drainage. In the summer the weather is extremely hot, and the breezes that blow in from the coast are warm. The humidity is high.

During the difficult economic times of the twenties and thirties, and even beyond, many men had to feed their families any way they could. They grew corn and used some of it for the best cash crop they could produce. That was moonshine liquor.

This is the story of one man who lived in that place at that time, and produced that product. It is also the story of his family, his children, and grandchildren. It is the story of survival, suffering, heartache, and tragedy.

There were good times, difficult times, hard times, and worse times. Not all of them survived the times. They died along the way, sometime in natural ways, and sometimes in tragic ways.

I was married to Lawrence Earl "Chief" McKenzie's son Jesse. I knew my father-in-law and mother-in-law well. We lived for forty years just down Levy Road from where Chief and his wife Leona lived. The story I tell came from Chief, other family members, and from my own observations and experiences.

I hope the reading of this story will be enlightening and helpful. Whether or not it is I cannot say. I can only say it is the true story of a family.

Leona and Madiline Skilling

Two

L awrence Earl McKenzie was born in an old house on a farm near Estill, South Carolina in Hampton County. The year was about 1895. He was the son of Mitchel Levi McKenzie. I do not know his mother's name. She died when Lawrence Earl was young, leaving him, brother George, and a sister. His father, a tall lanky man, then married a woman named Bertie. She and Mitchel Levi had two sons, Skeet and Alfred. That made a family of seven with five children.

The children went to a small country school where most likely all the pupils were in the same room with one teacher, which was the usual set-up in rural schools in those days. They learned the essential things, how to spell, read, write, and they learned their numbers. How much they learned of History, Science, Languages, and Current Events probably varied from school to school, community to community. In some of these small schools, subjects such as Latin, Algebra, French, and Spanish were taught. But these differences in curriculum probably depended on the education level of the teacher since there were no requirements for becoming one. Some teachers were college graduates, and others had only finished high school.

Lawrence Earl and George dropped out of school early to go to work, and help support the family. There is no record of what they did, but they likely worked on a nearby farm in order to earn some money to help the family along. It is obvious that their father agreed to this since this was a common occurrence at that time. They would not have made much money, but most things the family needed were cheap. Anything they made would have been a big help. So, the boys did what they could to help the family. Many children, especially boys, never finished school. There were no strict laws requiring children to stay in school and finish. They did what they had to do to survive. They worked on farms, or if they lived in cities they worked in mills and factories. There were no child labor laws. All members of a family made some kind of contribution to the family's well-being.

Most of what people in rural areas ate was grown by the family, but there were many things that had to be bought from a local store. These items would have been sugar, salt, flour, cloth, thread, buttons, just to name a few. Also, any items needed on the farm for work on houses had to be bought such as hammers, nails, saws, lumber, paint. So, there was the need of cash to make these purchases.

As a young man Lawrence worked on a Merchant Marine ship. America had managed to stay out of World

War I. It began in Europe in August, 1914 involving France, England, Belgium, Russia, Serbia, and Italy against Germany, Austria-Hungry, and Turkey. With the sinking of American cargo ships, and the sinking of a passenger ship, the Lusitania with a number of Americans on board, the United States was drawn into the war in 1917.

America's army was very small at the time, so a call for volunteers began. When this did not produce enough men, a draft was instituted.

Many men who did not want to fight in the trenches chose to join either the Navy or the Merchant Marines.

We do not have a record of Chief's service during this time, but this is likely when and why he enlisted. He would have been the right age, just over twenty. He served in the kitchen on a ship, and it is likely that is where he gained the name Chief. This may indicate that he worked his way up to being perhaps in charge of a kitchen, or at least had some responsibility beyond what others may have had.

As a seaman on a cargo ship, he would have made many trips to Europe as the United States supplied first England and France, and then its own Army stationed in France. This was dangerous duty. He may not have been in the foxholes and trenches of France, but there was every day the possibility of being sunk by a German submarine.

I cannot help but wonder what it was like to know that every night when you went to sleep you thought you might wake up on a sinking ship. The same thoughts and feelings would have been experienced during the day, especially for those working below deck with less chance of making it up to the top deck and a life-boat.

The war lasted much longer than anyone imagined, four long and difficult years. It had ground down to a state of armies facing each other across battlefields with neither side having an advantage. Then when the United States entered the war in 1917 the tide began to turn. The American Army was in several decisive battles that made all the difference causing the Germans to pull back.

Peace was finally reached on November 11, 1918, and a cease fire at 11:00 a.m. An Armistice was signed with Germany withdrawing its forces in defeat.

With the end of the war Chief was discharged at some point. He could have stayed in the Merchant Marines, and had a long career. It might not have been ideal, but at least it was a steady job. However Chief decided not to make that his life-long career. He managed to avoid the Spanish Flu which killed millions of people the world over. It may have been brought to

America by returning servicemen. He came back to South Carolina. But there the future was uncertain.

There were few choices for work when Chief came back home. One choice was to continue farm work, but he had no land of his own. There was not much future in being a dirt farmer. Being away during the war had opened up the world to him. He must have learned there are other ways to live than digging in the dirt, fighting the elements, and hoping a good crop would come in. That was no way to live and raise a family. He knew about living on the edge of poverty if not all the way in it. He was determined to find a better way.

Chief must have saved some money during the war. There was nowhere to spend it on board ship. He bought a store in Furman, South Carolina, a small settlement up the Savannah River in Hampton County, to the north-west of Savannah, Georgia. Furman was not far from where he had grown up, so he was familiar with that area. It was an old un-painted building beside the railroad track. He sold groceries, clothing, shoes, and hardware. The population of Furman in 1920 was 296. By 1930 it has shrunk to 270.

It was a farming area in a time when poverty was the norm. But many people did not know they were poor. They all thought their lot in life was just what it was supposed to be. They did not know any better, so they made do as they could with what they had.

The store was the kind of place where old men sat around on benches or old worn-out chairs outside in front, told stories, made their complaints, and spit tobacco juice out as far as they could. There may have been a large Coke sign on the side of the building, and little snuff and tobacco signs on the front windows or on the two old doors that swung open, and stayed open unless it was cold. The flies and other bugs were free to come and go as they pleased. If a stray bird flew in it would not stay long. An old stray dog might have wandered in looking for something to eat, and he might have found it or been given something. Then he may have been told to go home, but he probably just went outside and found a place in the shade of a tree.

Local people were in and out of the store, though not enough of them to make any store owner rich. They were able to purchase what they needed, and also catch up on any news or local gossip. Often the gossip was far more interesting than any news that came along.

Each afternoon a girl on her way home from school walked by Chief's store. He could not help but notice her. Often, she would go inside for candy and soft drinks. He would talk to her about school and her day. She would ask him about the store, and how it was going. She was showing an interest in him, and he was taken by her. He flirted with her, and she with him. Her name was Becky.

Chief told me he kept telling her she was too young to have a boyfriend. But it was not long before Becky and Chief were courting. Soon they were married. She had wanted to be with an older man.

She quit school, and became a house wife. She also helped out with the store. They lived in a small apartment in the back of the store, so it was very convenient for both of them.

Chief indicated to me this was his second marriage, though he never told me the name of his first wife or anything about the situation. Perhaps he had been married before the war, and his being away had ended that marriage. It is also possible that his opening the store in Furman and moving there had created a serious problem that could not be overcome.

Unknown to Chief, and even perhaps to Becky, she had a weak heart, and should not have had children. But Chief and Becky did not consider this evidently.

In those days most folk in the country had very little medical knowledge or access to it.

⚬

It was not long until Becky had a daughter they named Sallie Mae. That child was about two months old when Becky became pregnant with another child.

I do not know who named Sallie Mae, but Chief was at a loss for a name when the second daughter was born. One day he was putting canned peaches on the shelves in his store. He saw on the cans the words Alberta Peaches. So, there was his second daughter's name, Alberta.

During this time, they still lived in the back of the store, the situation for many people who owned small stores. Other store owners lived in large houses, and had a store in the house or in a side building.

Becky took care of the girls, kept house, and she also continued to help out with the store. The choices of where they could live were few or none. Even if there were other opportunities for housing the chances of them having enough money to afford some other place were non-existent.

⚬

Every week Chief would catch the train when it stopped by his store, and ride over to Savannah, Georgia where he would shop for goods at Alexander Wholesale Groceries. There were no companies that delivered groceries to stores, at least not that far out in the rural areas. The Southern Railroad ran a train that was called "Southern Columbia to Savannah Route". It made stops at all the little towns and communities along its route. Chief certainly had no other reliable transportation for the trip into Savannah. Taking the train was not only sensible, but was his only choice. So, he would go to the wholesale company, pick out all the things on his list, and then he would get them ready to take home. After his shopping was completed, he would gather what he had purchased, go back to the train station, board the train, and return home around midnight or later. But one of those days was not like any of the others.

It was the usual Saturday morning when he got up, and caught the early morning train to Savannah as he always did. He left Becky to watch the store and the girls just like every Saturday. The train of course did not come back through Furman until past midnight. When he got back home, he could hear the babies.

Chief told me, "I brought the goods in, put them

down on the floor, and heard the two babies crying. When I went in the bedroom, I thought Becky was sleeping and not hearing the babies. I fixed bottles for both of them. After giving them their bottles, I changed them, and then I put them to bed for the night. I then went in to wake Becky, and speak to her. I put my hand on her and shook her, but she was cold and did not move. She was dead.

"She was not supposed to take aspirin unless the doctor said to. But she had taken several out of a bottle on her bedside table.

"I was devastated by that. I called Becky's mother to come and get the girls."

Her funeral was held a day or two later, and she was buried in the family plot.

That tragic death left Chief with the two girls to raise. But Becky's mother helped take care of them because he could not do all that needed to be done and run the store.

Years later Sallie Mae and Berta told me they thought for years that Chief had left the aspirin so Becky would take them.

One day they confronted him, and asked, "Did you kill our mother?"

He replied, "No, and I'm sorry you lost your mother so young. I found her dead when I got back from

Savannah from buying goods for the store. It seems she had taken some aspirin when she went to bed, and died in her sleep."

—⁓—

A man with two children and a store to run cannot live alone very long without a help-mate.

At some point Chief married for a third time. He did not tell me the name of the woman. He only said she told him she had no children. After they were married, he found out she had three children. Eventually that marriage ended, and like the first one I have no information about it. Perhaps the two ready-made families just did not mix.

But he would not be single for long.

Leona Skilling

Three

It was apparently not long until Chief married Leona Skilling. That brought about a move into the southern tip of the lowcountry. In the early 1920s Chief built his house on Levy Road, which runs off U. S. Highway 17 about five miles below Hardeeville, South Carolina. It was just down from what is called the Y where a fork in the road leads to Bluffton and Hilton Head. He had a natural talent for carpentry work, and one that was needed in those days. Many people had to learn to do whatever they could to have a place to live. He bought an old building, probably a barn, in Estill, South Carolina, tore it down, and hauled the lumber to the site on Levy Road. He had bought several acres along the road as the site for his house, and eventually other houses. There were pine trees on the land as well as tall grass and weeds. Once cleared the property was a good place for a house and a large garden out on the back of the lot.

It was a comfortable house for the time with three bedrooms, a living room, kitchen, dining room, bathroom, and back porch. In that house lived Chief, his wife Leona, and eventually six children.

It is obvious that the store was not making a good enough living for him and his children or he would not have closed it up and left it. He may have sold it to someone which would have made the move easier to make. From somewhere he obtained the money to buy the Levy Road property.

When Chief married Leona Skilling, that made her his fourth wife. She was ten years younger than he was, and had been raised in what was called the back woods. She had three sisters and a brother. Their parents had moved the family to the Levy Turn Bridge area of Jasper County. Her father had been a policeman in Charleston, South Carolina, but decided to move the family to a rural area.

Of course, Chief brought with him his two daughters into this marriage, Sallie Mae and Berta. There were the usual problems and issues experienced by a blended family. But they all made the best of the situation.

Then over several years Chief and Leona had four children. That made the six children in that house.

First born was Lawrence Earl McKenzie, Jr. He had a dark complexion and black hair. He was called Monkey. He was born in 1925.

Next came another son Jesse Leon who was fair and blond, known as Jiggs. He was born in 1926. His curly hair turned dark when he was about eight years old.

The third child was a daughter named Wyona, born

in 1927. She was a small child with black hair, blue eyes, and very bright.

The fourth child was a daughter named Elizabeth. I think she was born the next year. She was not healthy at her birth, and stayed in the hospital the first six months of her life. Perhaps something happened at her birth that caused her to have issues from the time she was a child.

In the early 1930s the entire country was struggling during the Great Depression. There were no jobs. Businesses failed. Farms went bust. In the great cities people stood in bread lines in order to feed their families. In rural areas farmers did what they could to raise enough food to live on. A man with six children to feed would do almost anything for them. Chief McKenzie did what he could to put food on the table.

He had enough land to have a fine garden. He began raising all kinds of vegetables in it. But still the lack of money threatened their existence.

At some point unknown to me or anyone else he began making moonshine down in the swamps along the Savannah River. He was able to drive his truck down through the woods near the river, but then would have to walk further in to get to places where he would not be seen or found. He carried in on his back all that he needed, which would have been some kind of drum to cook the mash over a fire, tubing, something to catch the liquid when it came through the tubing, and then bottles and jugs. There was plenty of firewood available. He was deep enough in the swamp to keep anyone from being concerned about the rising smoke or the odor of the mash as it cooked. He was smart enough to go where he would not be discovered by local law enforcement officers or federal revenue agents who were always on the look-out for suspicious smoke rising above the horizon. They knew many people were making illegal whisky, and were anxious to catch them.

During prohibition this had become a very profitable cash crop. With no liquor for sale legally people resorted to whatever they could think up. Some smuggled it into cities like Savannah, Georgia from places like Canada, Mexico, and Cuba. Other people resorted to making their own most often in secluded places in the mountains of north Georgia and the Carolinas, and also in hard-to-reach rural areas along the coast and in the flat lands. This was true not only in the south but throughout the country. Some of it was made in towns and cities, but the chance of being detected was greater in those places.

With the end of prohibition alcohol was once again sold legally. The election of Franklin D. Roosevelt had hastened this development since he was against prohibition. There was just too much money to be made for the government with taxes on these sales of alcohol products. So, this meant the government wanted alcohol to be sold for the tax revenue it would bring in. But non-tax paid alcohol was not allowed. To sell it was cheating the government out of tax money it could have collected on legal alcohol. People who sold non-tax paid alcohol were therefore seen as criminals, and could be arrested and sent to prison if they were caught.

However, there were many people who preferred moonshine liquor because it was cheaper since no taxes were collected on it. It was also convenient and readily available. They cared nothing about the government and its restrictions.

The term moonshine comes from Scotland and Ireland where illegal liquor was first made because of excise laws. The first use of that word to describe illegal liquor appeared in 1785 in Grose's Dictionary of the Vulgar Tongue in the British Isles. It was most likely made only at night in secluded places giving it the name moonshine. That beverage was made with barley. In the United States it was made with corn mash.

With a Scottish heritage and a name like McKenzie, Chief must have naturally thought of making moonshine. It had a long history, especially in the south. He probably grew up knowing about it. A desperate man will use what knowledge and resources he has. So, Chief turned to what he knew.

He cooked in large barrels a mash made of corn, malt, syrup, and a lot of sugar. Many things could be added to make the mash rot and ferment such as fruits and vegetables. Many people in those days added things that were either unsavory or dangerous like dead animals. Some people used old automobile radiators which meant some anti-freeze got into the mix, and that made it deadly. If a squirrel or a rat out of curiosity fell into the mash that could not be helped. But Chief did not knowingly use anything like that. It was just lots of corn, sugar, the other ingredients, and fruits.

He always cooked at night because he figured the law enforcement people would be at home asleep during those hours. They likely would not have gone off into the swamps at night looking for a still unless they had an idea where one was.

When the fires heated up and the mash began to cook a sweet aroma would drift up into the air. This would often attract visitors. Those swampy areas along the river were filled with all kinds of animals. Snakes would often crawl by. Possums and racoons would come sneaking up. They were night creatures, and were out rambling around looking for whatever they could find.

One cold winter night as he sat by the fire, Chief heard a noise behind him. He slowly turned around, and there was a large black bear standing up on its hind legs looking over the bushes. That sweet odor had brought him up near the fire. But the bear did not have the nerve to come any closer to the fire and this human he was looking at. He finally turned around, and went away. Chief was mighty glad he left.

It was not unusual for there to be deaths caused by poison in moonshine. There were numerous incidents where people would be together, perhaps at a party, and several would die after drinking poison moonshine.

A safe product attracted more customers and created a good reputation. That must have made

Chief's moonshine desirable for his was safe. He was careful to not have anything in his that was dangerous or harmful.

There are no records of course of how he started selling his product or to whom, but most likely he just sold it locally. He may have sold it to a person he knew who would then tell others where he got it. It would not have taken long for the word to get around. Like in most things, success breeds success.

Things were going well for Chief McKenzie. In a time of economic difficulty, he was making a good living for, not only his family, but began to see how he could for a few others as well.

Perhaps he thought there must be a way to expand what he was doing. If he could make a living off of moonshine, then maybe he could make an even better living off more moonshine. He had found out there was certainly a market for his product. Even those who had very little money would find a way to satisfy their thirst. He knew alcohol would always be a product with a clientele. But how could he best expand his market? He had to find a way to supply more people than just the ones he knew around his area. There was only so much potential for that. He came upon an idea.

Leona Skilling

Four

A s things began to look up Chief decided to expand his business. He opened a night club where he could sell his product.

Chief must have known about night clubs in Savannah, and surely some of them were his customers. But he also knew there were none in Jasper County. There may have been some small roadside beer joints after alcohol was again legal, but in the lower part of the county there were none. This meant that anyone in the county who wanted to go to a club had to travel over into Savannah. A shrewd businessman would surely see there was an opportunity in that situation. A new local night club would be a lot closer for men in Jasper County as well as those who lived just across the river. They could reach that new club much quicker than driving into Savannah.

The new club was located on Highway 17 just before a vast area of marsh and savannas a few miles before the Savannah River and the town of Port Wentworth, Georgia. That area is now a wildlife refuge. He hired nine young ladies from Georgia and South Carolina. The club was in a two-story building. So, not only increased alcohol sales, but now a new avenue for making his moonshine available. The waitresses worked down-stairs. Some of these young ladies who worked at the club also made moonshine deliveries.

Chief worked there at night, and Leona worked

there in the day-time while he slept at home. However, she did not like this idea of running this night club, and they fought about it most of the time. It was probably not the alcohol sales she objected to, but the young ladies serving it and working with Chief. She obviously did not like that part of the business. It was just a step too far for her. The moonshine was one thing. She understood why he had to take that step. It made a living for them, but this other part, running the club, was just too much. She would not have it any longer than she had to. There was a confrontation over that coming at some point in the not too distant future.

With both of them working something had to be done to take care of the children. Young Black girls were hired to watch after the four younger children during the day. Sallie Mae and Berta could pretty well take care of themselves.

There was an older Black woman who lived across the field from where the McKenzie home is located. Many years after all this I often saw her walking down Levy Road. Whenever she saw me in the yard she would stop and talk for a while. She had been a baby sitter for the children when they were young. She said there was always trouble in the house, "lots of fussing and fighting".

Chief began taking home with him some of the young ladies who had worked all night so they could rest during the day. It was said to be, "out of the goodness of his heart".

It was not long until Leona became suspicious about that arrangement. So, one morning she decided to go home just to check on things. All hell broke loose it was said.

That was a near breaking point.

During most of their time together Chief and Leona did not get along. Perhaps her background, along with his behavior, added to their problems. She was raised by a father said to be a sick and curt man, but her own behavior was often mean and cruel. She must have taken after him in the way she treated people.

I was told Leona and a sister would put sheets over their heads, go to a window outside, and scare the children who were inside until they would scream and hide under the bed. Sallie Mae and Berta would try to console them while Leona and her sister were outside laughing.

Leona would throw things at the children. One day

she hit Sallie Mae in the back with a clock. Sallie Mae picked the clock up, and threw it back at her. Then she called her grandmother, Becky's mother, and asked her to come get her and Berta. Once they were away from there, they never went back to live with Leona and Chief again.

It was not long until Sallie Mae married a man named F. W. Zorn, a farmer in Estill, South Carolina where she and Berta had gone to live. By the age of eighteen Sallie Mae had three children. She was a crafty, talented person. She made the children's clothes for them as well as curtains and anything else they needed.

On the farm they raised peanuts, cotton, corn, as well as raising cows. The farm consisted of hundreds of acres. Also, Sallie Mae had her own garden where she raised vegetables. They lived in a large country home which had been in his family dating back to the 1800s and belonged to his great grandfather.

Being such a sweet and caring person Sallie Mae helped take care of F. W.'s parents until they died.

As time went on Sallie Mae learned that F. W. would borrow money to plant the crops, and then when he made money on the harvest, he would not pay off the loans. He would just pay the interest. Instead of paying the loans off he would buy new cars, trucks, and an airplane one year. This went on for many years.

Sallie Mae began having health problems. She spent a lot of time in a hospital in Columbia, South Carolina. By then their children were grown and on their own.

Finally, one year when F. W. went to the bank to get a loan for planting season the bank refused to let him have the money. They foreclosed on the farm and the house.

Sallie Mae and F. W. moved into a small trailer where he would leave her from time to time. But still he would always come back to her.

F. W. died of kidney disease, leaving Sallie Mae alone. Even though he was not a good husband she depended on him a great deal, and was lost without him. She spent her final years in one nursing home after another.

Alberta, known as Berta to us, was tall. She was a smart young lady, finished school, and went to college. She also married a farmer. His name was Lucas Vaughn. They were married in Macon, Georgia. He owned and operated a farm near Hawkinsville, Georgia. He had a very large farm. In that part of the state the big money crops were peanuts, peaches, cotton, watermelon, and corn. Lucas Vaughn did very well. They had one son. She went to work at the Air Force base in Warner Robbins, Georgia. She worked there until she retired.

The two of them got along just fine though they had the usual issues most couples have. They must have worked things out very well for they were married for fifty years. In her later life she suffered from lupus.

Sallie Mae and Berta complained to their father until the day he died about Leona's attitude toward them because he would not say anything to stop her. They always thought he was afraid of her. But for them that was no excuse for they felt no one should ever let a spouse or anyone else be unkind to children.

It was good for them that they escaped Leona's wrath when they did. They at least had a chance of a better life.

Even though Chief dealt in moonshine liquor, one thing he never did, he never drank any moonshine. Though he never touched the stuff, the stuff touched his family in the worst way.

It is interesting that he felt that way about alcohol. What caused him to think this way? Was it something he saw when he was in the Merchant Marines? Or was it that he knew what his product did to people who bought it from him? If that is what it was, he certainly had no bad feelings or guilt because of what it did to those people.

What it did to his own family was something else however.

Leona Skilling and her mother

Five

C hief often kept gallon jugs of moonshine under the house. The jugs were made of various materials, and were of various designs and shapes. There were also quart jars. That way it could be kept relatively cool, and it was out of sight. It was readily available in case someone came by the house who wanted to buy a quart or more. Though it was under the house and hidden from everyone he thought, it was not completely hidden. The curiosity of boys sometimes gets the best of them. You may think you have hidden something from them, but they often have a way of finding things.

A tree is meant to be climbed. A creek is meant to be waded. A river is meant for swimming. A path in the woods is meant to be followed. And barns, sheds, and houses have the most alluring places meant to be explored.

It was said that Monkey (Lawrence Earl, Jr) and Jiggs (Jesse Leon) were not watched after very well. There was never enough food in the house for them. But their baby-sitters did the best they could for them. Their older half-sisters, Sallie Mae and Berta, had done what they could to help out with them before they left for good. They did this knowing that Leona despised them, and resented them being in their home since they were the products of one of Chief's earlier marriages.

The boys however were wild and unruly. They ran

loose all the time, running off in the woods, climbing trees and sheds.

One day, about the year 1933, when Monkey was eight years old and Jiggs was a year younger at seven, they decided under the house was a good place to explore.

Chief was asleep, having been up all night, and was not watching them. Leona of course was working. They probably both assumed the baby-sitters were keeping an eye on the boys.

It was not long until Monkey and Jiggs discovered the jugs and jars of moonshine. The curiosity of such a find was too much to be ignored. They opened a jar, and began tasting the contents. They had at first thought it was water, but then realized it was something else. Jiggs did not like it because it burned his mouth. But Monkey kept on drinking it, more and more. He drank so much that he soon passed out.

Around seven that evening Monkey fell into a deep sleep, and was rushed to a hospital in Savannah, Georgia about thirty minutes away. He was in a coma, and did not wake up. He died the next day. The doctors thought it was a brain hemorrhage. Chief and Leona knew it was alcohol poisoning. Neither of them mentioned to the doctors what the boys had done. No one ever told what had really happened until years later when Sallie Mae told the story. Chief must have been afraid if anyone found out what happened he would be prosecuted. Not only would he be charged with making moonshine, but more seriously he would probably have faced a charge of some degree of homicide.

I have seen photos of Monkey dressed in a little white suit lying in a pine casket. He looked like he was sleeping. He was such a handsome little boy with his dark complexion and black hair. He was laid to rest in the May River Church cemetery on a hot summer day in July.

Things were never the same in that family. I often wondered why Leona seemed to hate Chief so much. Looking back, I believe it was because Chief left that moonshine hidden under the house. Leona blamed Chief for Monkey's death. Maybe she was right. He should never have put it there.

After the death of Monkey Jiggs was lost. He never got over his brother's death. He talked about him up until his own death at the age of sixty-eight. He finally joined him in the May River Church cemetery.

Now without Monkey Jiggs turned to Wyona for

companionship. She was a year younger than Jiggs. One day they were out playing in the yard. Chief had built a large shed in the back. Leona had often told them not to climb up on it because they could get hurt. Since she was not there, they climbed up on top of it. It was about six o'clock in the evening, supper time. Soon they saw Leona pull in the driveway home from work. This scared them because Leona would often beat them for no reason. Soon she was calling them in to eat. As they were in a hurry to get down Jiggs pushed Wyona. She fell on a board with a nail sticking up from it, and it stuck in her knee. For the rest of her life, she had trouble with that leg. It did not develop as it should have.

At some point, after a period of several years, whether because of Monkey's death or because of her concern about the club Leona made a big decision. She was perhaps mad at Chief for not watching the boys and being asleep or being occupied otherwise. Whichever it was she took matters into her own hands.

She fired all the girls at the club, closed the doors, and locked them. She called the police, and reported the serving of moonshine liquor downstairs in the club. That was the end of it.

However, it was not the end of Chief's moonshine business. He came up with another good idea.

~~~

If Chief's night club was over, and that outlet for his product was gone, then he would have to find a way to expand his market. If he could no longer sell his moonshine in that location then he would find other locations. He was no longer satisfied with how he had begun. That was selling a few quarts and jugs here and there to people he knew. Once a man has made a lot of money, he can never go back to a small-time business.

Chief decided to branch out into a lucrative export business. That meant exporting beyond his local area to neighboring cities and states. Beyond the Hardeeville area Savannah, Georgia, across the river, would have been his first big target. He sold shipments of moonshine in not only Georgia, but also Florida, further up in South Carolina, and in North Carolina. This may well have included such cities as Brunswick, Georgia, Jacksonville, Florida, Charleston and Columbia, South Carolina, and Charlotte, North Carolina, as well as possibly Wilmington and Fayetteville.

There were many problems with all this. The major one being the government. Revenue agents were on constant alert looking for moonshiners in the woods, in the swamps, in the out of the way valleys with little creeks running through them. And they were always looking for suspicious automobiles that seemed to be carrying heavy loads. The cars might be tilted down in the back, and that was a dead giveaway. Often there were road-blocks and random checks. The agents would tell the drivers to pull over, and then begin searching their cars. It would not take long to find what they were looking for.

Chief was keenly aware of all this. He had to find a way to get around this problem, the problem of revenue agents and roadblocks. Maybe he thought the best way around a problem is always through it instead of around it.

Chief told me, "I had three pretty young girls who drove for me. Most of the time they were never stopped. But if they were, they would smile, talk sweet, and be on their way. That went on for many years."

No one would ever suspect a nice-looking young lady in a nice car to be hauling moonshine. The agents were keeping an eye out for rough looking men.

The fact that all this was successful is proven by the

kind of cars those young ladies drove. He always put them in new Buicks, Chevrolets, and Fords.

The money they made was more than they could make at any other job, if there had been any jobs for them in those days, for most women did not work until during and after World War II. It was not until then that women were common in the work place. Even then Chief paid his drivers more than they could make anywhere else. Because of what he paid them they could take care of their children and other family members. This was Chief's equal wage for women that set him apart from all other employers. He was a man far ahead of his time.

In this period Chief bought a lot of land, seeing it as a good investment. The price of land was very cheap in those days. Much of it was fifty dollars an acre. He bought parcels in both Jasper and Beaufort Counties. He was offered some land at a very cheap price on Hilton Head island, but turned down that opportunity saying, "That land over there ain't worth nothin'. It's nothin' but sand, and you couldn't grow anything on it."

That was one investment he should have made for the island of Hilton Head is now a vacation spot that attracts visitors from around the world as well as a place to retire for people from around the country. Millions of dollars could have been made by Chief if he had made that investment, but in those days, no one could ever have imagined what happened there, and the vast potential that existed.

Chief McKenzie

Six

D uring these years Chief and Leona's children were
growing up.

Jesse, or Jiggs as he was called, did not finish high
school. At the age of eighteen he joined the United
States Army Air Force, and was stationed for the most
part at Fort Worth, Texas. This was toward the end of
World War II.

While Jiggs was there, he met and then married a
young woman named Maxine. They had a daughter
named Darlene. When he was later discharged from
the Air Force, they came to his home in Hardeeville,
South Carolina. Jiggs went to work at American Can
Company. But the marriage did not last, and she went
back to Fort Worth, never to return to Hardeeville. They
soon divorced. There must have been some problems
other than her having to leave Texas and move to South
Carolina, but that was the last straw, I guess.

⁓

Wyona was Chief's and Leona's only child to finish
high school. She graduated from Hardeeville High
School. She had black hair and blue eyes, and stood
five feet and six inches tall, weighing one hundred
and thirty pounds. She married a man named Clayton
Rast, a Greyhound Bus driver.

She had met him on her many trips up to Estill to

see Sallie Mae. She would walk over to Highway 17, and catch the bus there. Some thought she made those trips just to get to see Clayton Rast.

The problem was he was married to a school teacher in Swansea, South Carolina, just south of Columbia. But the attraction for both of them was instant even though he was fourteen years older than she was. She was still a teenager about to finish school. He was a tall handsome man, and Wyona set her sights on him right off.

It was not long until he divorced his wife, and they were married. They lived in Cayce, South Carolina, near Columbia. They adopted a boy and a girl.

Clayton ran for the South Carolina House of Representatives several times, but he never won an election. During one of those races, he made a speech one night. After the gathering was over, he and Wyona walked outside to the car. He suddenly fell to one knee, and then fell over dead from a heart attack.

Wyona had a lawyer who got the insurance money she could have used to pay off the house they lived in. It was a clear case of theft, but nothing was ever done about it. She was alone and helpless, and did not know what to do.

Later she began seeing other men, and finally married one who was not a good influence on her. She began to smoke and drink at his insistence. She was apparently easily influenced by him.

Not long after they married, he tried to get my husband Jiggs to give him the old home place as payment for a lawyer's fee. But I tore up the paper into a hundred pieces, and mailed it back to him.

Wyona began a series of trips to the hospital. She would then go home, get better, and then get worse and return to the hospital. The doctors did not seem to know what was wrong with her. She died after a while. When I heard about her death, I called the hospital and asked them to do an autopsy. They told me her husband had already had her cremated.

Wyona was a good person, but was too trusting, and was taken advantage of by that man.

Elizabeth, called Liz, was their youngest child, and had life-long mental issues. She always had difficulty in school, even though her teachers tried to help her. She could never accomplish anything. When she was grown, she tried to work cleaning rooms at a local motel.

Then she came in one night, and said she was going to marry a man from North Carolina. The man had left his wife and two sons. He did not know anything about Liz's health history.

⸺⸱⸺

I came into this family in 1954 when I married Jiggs. I was working at Union Bag. My brother Gene worked at American Can Company where Jiggs also worked. One day Gene brought him home to meet me. The result was our marriage. My family lived in a large two-story house in what was called the Saw Mill Village. This was along the Savannah River, about a mile down a dirt road from Port Wentworth, Georgia. So, Jiggs and I lived with my parents, brother Gene, and sisters Pat and Shirley, and my son Danny from a previous marriage.

⸺⸱⸺

The Saw Mill Village was a quaint place. All the houses there were large. The streets were dirt, being unpaved. There were tall oak trees along the streets covered in Spanish moss. The children played all over the village, and every mother kept an eye out for all of them. There was no danger for them or anyone else in the village.

We all enjoyed living in the big house, but there was also the desire to have a place of our own.

So, in 1957 we built a house on a lot which was a part of the Levy Road property owned by Chief. He gave us the lot. My parents also built a house next to ours.

Both houses were made of concrete blocks. They had the usual kitchen, living room, three bedrooms, and one bathroom.

It was living in the country with plenty of room for gardens. We planted on both lots fruit trees and shrubs.

After a time, our grandmother, who was my Mom's mother, moved onto our land in a small house built for her. We called her Granny Gray. She was a small woman, and was very wise.

We all enjoyed the feeling of the country atmosphere with lots of room for the adults, and also for the children to play anywhere and everywhere. My sisters Shirley and Pat went to school in Hardeeville, as did my children and those of Liz. But there was a drawback about moving there. That threw us into the drama always surrounding Liz and the rest of the family.

Jiggs and I had a son named Donny, and then a daughter named Angela.

As our children got older, I decided I wanted to work

again. I opened a truck stop cafe on Highway 17, just up from Levy Road. It was a popular place with truckers and business was good. This was in the days before I-95 was built, and Highway 17 was still the main road from upper South Carolina down into Georgia. Not only truckers, but other people as well would stop in for a good meal, among them country singer Tom T. Hall and his band and Burt Reynolds.

I hired several of the Black ladies I knew to work for me. They were loyal and hard-working. I slept in the day-time, and worked at night. Our business was growing, and our reputation spread up and down Highway 17. Truckers especially would share with each other good places to stop. They wanted good country type cooking and good service. We supplied both.

Liz's odd behavior continued during these years and became worse. The man she married was a Marine. They had three children, one boy and two girls. Their names were Joseph, Mona Marie, and Deborah Ann. After some time, her husband disappeared, and apparently went back to North Carolina. I do not know if he had been stationed at Paris Island in South Carolina, near Beaufort and Hardeeville, and then went to Camp Lejeune in North Carolina. Both places were

Marine bases. All of those details are lost, but this is most likely what happened.

The family was left with Liz and her three children. She was totally incapable of taking care of them. She could not even take care of herself, much less anyone else. So, it fell to the rest of us to pitch in and do what we could.

We can only imagine what it was like for her husband to live with Liz. A person can only take so much. But no man should go off, and leave his children like that. He obviously did not love her enough and love them enough to try to stay, and help them all. Of course, this is looking at the situation only from my point of view. But they were his children. He brought them into this world, and he should have at least supported them in some way, instead of abandoning them.

Our children, Danny, Donny, and Angie grew up with Joe, Mona, and Deborah.

Danny said that one time he, Donny, and Joe were playing in Monkey John Swamp. They discovered a still, and were immediately afraid the moonshiner might get them. Anyone finding a still was in danger from those who ran it. But did that still belong to Chief? They had many such adventures.

⁓

Liz's condition continued to become more serious over time.

When Liz had emotional episodes, the Sheriff would often be called to pick her up, and take her to the state mental hospital in Columbia, South Carolina. At other times Chief would take her there. She was in and out of that hospital for years and years. They, of course, attempted to treat her, but nothing they ever did seemed to do her any good for long.

With Liz unable to take care of her children Chief and Leona and other family members stepped in to provide for them. But this was sometime difficult for Leona.

⁓

Leona's sister lived across the road from her and Chief. She was Aunt Jack to all of us. She was a wonderful person. She bought clothes for Liz's children, took them to church, and gave them food. Her husband Lawrence owned a service station up Highway 17 in

Hardeeville, South Carolina. It was good to have them nearby so they could help keep an eye on the situation, and especially look out for the children since they ran all over the area.

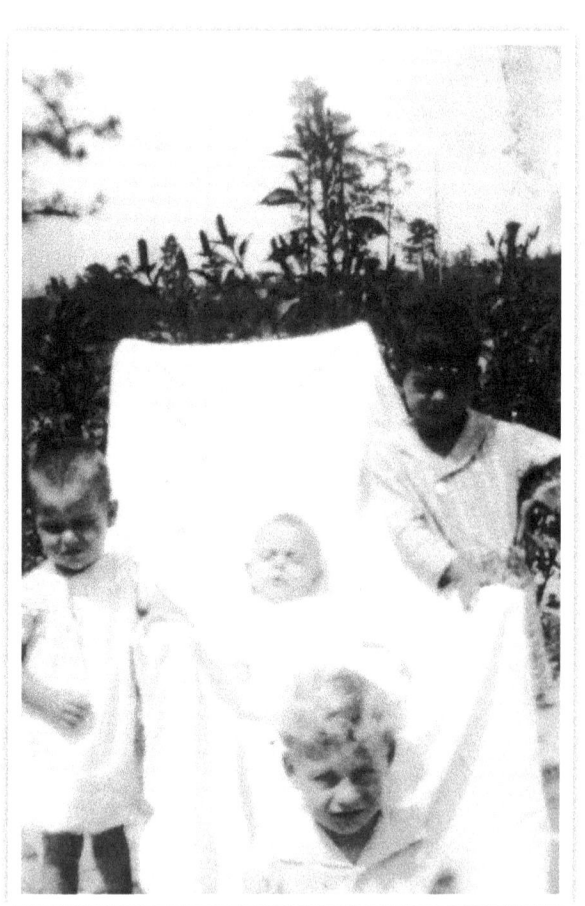

Jess, Wyona, Liz, and Monkey, back right

Seven

S ince Leona had no patience with children, it was a hard life for all three of them. They never stood a chance. Joe being the boy and the oldest had a particularly difficult time. Leona would grab a switch, a cord, or a limb, and beat those children. One day she was beating Joe in my yard. I went outside when I saw it, grabbed him away from her, and took him inside. I began to realize how serious Leona's mental problems were.

When Joe was eight years old Leona put him in an orphanage, probably because he was too unruly for her, and also because she did not want him around.

Most of the boys in the orphanage were older than Joe was. Naturally, or maybe unnaturally, Joe was a target for them. It was easy for them to pick on him. They made a game out of tormenting him. He would come home for a visit from time to time, and was always bruised and beaten. He told me they would wrap him up in a sheet, and push him down the stairway. This was no place for a child. He was worse off there than he was at home. I do not know why anyone would allow other large boys to mistreat a child in this way when he was there to be taken care of.

I decided to put a stop to that. I sent Jiggs to go to the orphanage, and pick up his clothes and other belongings.

I told Jiggs, "They are not putting him into that orphanage again. Go get his chest of drawers, and bring it and him here."

I moved him into our house to live with our two boys, Danny and Donny. Leona did not like that, but I did not care. It was far past time to do something to help that child.

In spite of his unruly behavior Joe was the easy come and easy go type. He was a handsome boy I grew to love as though he was my own son. He reminded me so much of Monkey, dark hair and dark complexion.

One day Joe and my son Donny were off playing in the woods. They were teenagers by then. They went down an old logging road and found a county owned bull-dozer. It was just sitting there. Being boys looking for something to get into they knew they had found it. They managed to hot-wire it, crank it up, and drive it around. They bulldozed anything and everything that got in their way. Those two had many such adventures. I knew about many of them, but there is no telling what they got into that I never heard about. Maybe it is good that I did not know everything they did.

In spite of what I or anyone else could do for Joe it seemed he was destined for a difficult time as he grew older and became an adult.

Joe stayed with us until he was eighteen years old. He decided he wanted to join the Navy. That was a good idea for him. Danny joined the Marines, so Joe may have gotten the idea because of that. Whatever the reason it gave Joe a chance to learn something he might have been able to use later on.

He had bought a black Mustang. Before he left for the Navy he was driving up to Hardeeville. A Coco-Cola truck pulled in front of him, hitting him head-on. That threw Joe out of the front windshield and over the hood, breaking both of his legs. Since he was already enlisted in the Navy, he was put in the Navy hospital at Paris Island. After his recovery he then went on active duty.

Being in the Navy was good for Joe. It gave him some stability, discipline, and guidance. He greatly needed these things, since so much of his life had been without them.

After serving his time he came home and worked several jobs, never staying very long with any of them.

The longest time was at Great Dane Trailer Company in Savannah.

He married and he and his wife had two children.

One evening he came to check on Liz, Chief, and Leona. He went in the back screen porch door, and called out "Hello". He walked through the house, called out, "Anyone home?" But he found no one. Then he looked in Liz's bedroom, and found her on the floor. She had found a gun they thought was hidden. She had put the gun in her mouth, and pulled the trigger. It blew off the back of her head. It fell to Joe to clean up the room.

If all he had been through all his life was not enough, this was an experience terrible enough to shake anyone and scar them for life.

At some point he began smoking marijuana. I do not know when this began whether when he was in the Navy or after he came back home. I also do not know if he began using other drugs. But whatever he used this put him in contact with the worst kind of people for he had to buy what he used from somebody, and those who sold any drugs were not the cream of the crop kind of folk.

One Friday night he went to the home of a drug dealer. While he was there, he was robbed. He left, and went to borrow a shot-gun from someone. He went back to that house, shot at a mattress on the floor, and hit the drug dealer. Those in the house were afraid to call for help, then finally did, but it was too late. He bled to death.

Joe was arrested, and put in jail. When his case came to trial, he had no lawyer. He was given a public defender. I went to the courthouse in Ridgeland, South Carolina. His lawyer said as court was about to begin, "Which one is Joe Gibbs?" He had never even talked to Joe. There was another Gibbs there facing charges, and this lawyer did not know one from the other. When the proceedings began, I raised my hand, and asked to speak. The judge allowed me to do so. I told how our sheriff had been on television, channel 11 in Savannah, and said where the dealer lived was a crack house. The sheriff had known it for two years. I asked, "If he had known it why didn't he shut it down?" The judge said I was right, and asked why? Then the judge said, "Joe Gibbs, how do you plead?" His defender said, "Guilty." Joe had not ever even met the man before, certainly they had not discussed his plea. He was given a life sentence.

Joe has been in jail over twenty-five years. They will not let him speak at his hearings.

Mona, Liz's middle child, was a sweet girl. But when she grew up, she did not always make good choices in the men she was with. Finally, when she married, she and her husband had two children, a girl and a boy.

Much later on Mona would come to our house, and ask for money. She would tell me how hungry she was, and ask for food I had on the stove.

The last time she came to see me a man was sitting outside in his truck. She was black and blue from having been beaten. I told her I was going to call the sheriff to come get him, and for her to sit down and wait. She left, and I never saw her again.

I was told she went to see her sister Deborah up north, and asked to stay with her. Deborah had turned her down several times before, but this time she was sick. She soon went in the hospital, and died of ovarian cancer. The poor girl had no life.

Deborah was Liz's youngest daughter. She was a pretty girl, and was always well-dressed when she grew up. She had a couple of difficult marriages.

One day she showed up at my house and wanted to stay with me until she could find a place to rent in South Carolina, having left where she was in Georgia. But she did not stay long. She moved away and I lost track of her.

With the mother they had and the start they had in life it is a wonder Joe, Mona, and Deborah did not turn out worse than they did, and have a worse time than they had.

I felt like I did what I could for them as they grew older, but I also know I could only do so much. They could not overcome their family heritage or their environment. They never had much of a chance in life, but still even at that people have to take responsibility for their own well-being and the paths they choose to follow.

Monkey

Eight

There came a time when the moonshine business was no longer profitable. It was also a dangerous thing to be involved in. Aside from that it involved a lot of hard work, and Chief was too old to keep it up.

At that point he began working for his brother George who lived in Savannah, Georgia.

The Colony of Georgia and the City of Savannah were established on a bluff twenty miles up the river from the coast in February, 1733. The leader of the settlers was James Oglethorpe. The Trustees of the colony created it in order to have a place for debtors to live. Many of them had been put in prison in England. However less than half of the settlers were debtors, though most all of them were poor.

There were certain restrictions put in place for this new colony. There was to be no rum, brandy, or any alcohol allowed. There were to be no lawyers. There were to be no slaves owned there, but they could be borrowed from South Carolina. And finally, there was to be freedom of religion, except no Catholics were allowed. The fear was they would be loyal to the Pope and the Spanish in Florida. Spain had settled Florida, and sought to expand its territory.

Over time these restrictions faded away. There were many slaves in Georgia. There are now many lawyers in Savannah, and a great deal of alcohol. Sometime the two mix. As for religion there is a strong Catholic population in Savannah as well as other denominations and religions of all sorts.

There was another reason the founding of Georgia was favored so by so many. England wanted to establish a buffer between Florida and South Carolina. So, it was not only out of a good heart and compassion that the city and colony were founded. It was also out of concern for the safety of South Carolina.

Savannah has always been a thriving economic center for the coastal region, including the lowcountry of South Carolina. Whenever people in the lowcountry spoke of going to town there was only one place they were referring to, Savannah. That was always the case, and is still today.

There is still one thing that remains throughout the centuries and decades. Savannah still has its share, or more than its share, of debtors and the poor. For these people George McKenzie met a need. He offered cheap housing in cheap houses in poor neighborhoods. While Savannah was a place that was thriving, there were so many people there who were just hanging on by their finger-nails.

I never knew much about Chief's two half-brothers. I know both of them married. Skeet and his wife lived in Florida. I do not know where Alfred and his wife lived. I do know they had one daughter, but I am not sure if Skeet and his wife had any children. But I knew a lot about George and his business interests.

George owned a lot of property and several businesses.

He was in the pulpwood business, and was also a contractor. In addition to those he owned several old grocery stores he rented out to people, and had a lot of rental property.

George was married, and they had several children. But he left his first wife, and married his secretary. They had three boys.

Eventually George began to have some financially difficult times as he grew older and began losing what he had. It was at that point that Chief went to work for him.

Part of Chief's job was repair work on the rental houses George owned. All of them were in the poor areas of Savannah. He did work on porches and doors, windows and closets, painting, plumbing repairs under them, whatever needed to be done.

One day he came home from work later than usual. He came stumbling in the house, holding his head. He had been working under a house on the plumbing. When he crawled out from under it someone hit him on the head. Maybe the person thought he had a lot of money on him, which he did not have. He never knew who did it. But for a month he could not walk or drive a car.

Whenever a person gave up and closed down a store it would be Chief's job to go clean it out. He would take my son Donny and nephew Joe with him to help him. They would bring home bags of old-fashioned candy, Green Apples and Mary Janes, as well as other brands. I am not sure what happened to other things that were in those stores. Maybe he brought those things home as well.

Then there was the day when Chief came home, and said George was in the hospital. He was not sure what was wrong with him. He was seriously ill though, Chief knew that. He soon died. No one ever knew or will ever know what happened.

Whatever the cause of George's death that ended all his businesses. It also was the end of Chief's working in Savannah. No longer having a job he stayed around his property, and passed his time with his own repair work and gardening.

Chief had built a large shed out back much earlier. For years he had stored all kinds of things in it. During this time when he worked for George, he brought home from the work in Savannah left-over lumber, doors, windows, nails, hardware, plumbing, anything and everything. All of these items would have gone to waste or been thrown away. So, Chief put them to good use, knowing that at some point he would need many of these things. Some of them he would never use, but he was prepared for anything that happened.

One day he was up on top of the shed and got too hot. He was seventy-two years old at the time. This had happened several times before. But this time it was more serious. Leona heard a noise out back. When she looked out, she saw him lying down on the ground. She thought he was having a heart attack. When she reached him, she realized it was not that, but still the heat had gotten to him. She made him sit in the swing attached to a large limb of a sycamore tree. She ran and got some cool cloths, and applied them to his face and head. She wanted him to go to the doctor, but as usual he refused, saying he would be okay in a few minutes.

Leona managed to get him in the house where he took a bath and cooled down. His heavy work clothes which he always wore were ringing wet. For several days he did not go back outside to work. He sat in his chair in the living room reading the paper.

Having gotten over this episode he continued to do his outside chores, and his work in his garden. He had a large tractor he used to plow up his garden area every spring. In it he grew tomatoes, beans, corn, okra, and onions. Everyone in the family would warn him about getting too hot out in the sun, but he kept on anyway.

He did all the grocery shopping at the L & A Grocery store across the river in Port Wentworth, Georgia. Then he would share what he bought, paper products and other items, and always of course whatever he grew in his garden.

Whenever Chief bought a car, he paid cash for it. He would drive them until they wore completely out. I remember one old black Buick he drove until the interior cloth in the ceiling was hanging down.

Now with George gone and Chief retired, I saw a lot more of him because of that. He would come walking down Levy Road to our house, and come in the door talking and smoking. He talked a lot about politics. I am not sure he knew much about that subject, but he could spend half a day talking about it. He sat at the bar which was between our den and kitchen, and smoked one cigarette after another. I could hardly breath, and I would send the children out to play.

I remember so well many of the things I heard him say.

"You only need the knee cessities of life."

"By jingo the luck."

"You never know what's around the next corner."

"Treat people like you want to be treated."

"You're only as good as your word."

"What goes around comes around."

"I have no personal advice on life as I made so damn many mistakes myself."

He would also tell stories about the old days, and his earlier life. He had many varied experiences. It was during these conversations that I learned so much about the things that happened when he was young.

Chief was good to our children, and from the day she was born called our daughter Angie his little Angelo. Our son Donny kept Chief's old brown felt hat after he was gone, and wore it sometime. The hat was so old it had holes in it.

Leona had a stroke, and was unable to speak. But one day she came running down the road pointing to the garden, crying, trying to scream. Jiggs saw her, and ran up to the house. He found Chief lying face down in the garden.

Some men with South Carolina Power Company saw what was happening. They ran over to try and help, but nothing could be done. But they picked him up, took him in the house, and placed him on his bed. The Chief had died in his garden.

Several years later Leona had another stroke, this time a fatal one.

The Chief of lowcountry moonshine was gone. It was the end of him, and the end of an era. The old homeplace has never been the same, and neither has Levy Road.

With the passing away of each generation something is lost. With them goes the way they lived, the things they believed, the history they made, and the impact of their lives. For some people some of that was bad and damaging. For others many things were good and helpful. But whichever it was it affected the way coming generations lived and thought of themselves. It remains to be seen what the lasting affect will be on those lives they touched with their lives.

Do the people Chief McKenzie knew still remember

him? What happens when they are gone? What will remain of him or any of us?

Do the bears, coons, and snakes in the swamps wonder where he has gone? Do the foxes turn their noses up in the wind and fail to catch the smell of cooking corn? Do the old trees sway in the breeze, look down, and see nothing in the little clearings now?

It was a different time and a different circumstance, but the indelible impressions of the time and the people remain the same. Nothing will ever be again like it was then. Perhaps some of it we will like to call back. Perhaps there is much we would not want to see, experience, learn of ever again. But the history of every family is what it is. No one can go back and change anything. We cannot add to or take away. We can only say these were people who were merely human, those strange creatures that are a combination of so many things.

If this was true of anyone it was true of Chief McKenzie and his family. The Moonshine Chief lived and died, and the generations followed after him.

The End

Joe Gibbs

Lenoa and Chief McKenzie

Books by Tom Pilgrim

Fiction

In The Heat Of Texas
The Taste Of Paradise

Non-fiction

Faith For Today And Tomorrow
The Master Has Come
The Roads Jesus Traveled
Behold The Man
The Man From Galilee
They Came Together In Bethlehem
The Light Of Bethlehem Shines On

Lightning Source UK Ltd.
Milton Keynes UK
UKHW012020060521
383282UK00007B/676/J